Gerardo Gacharná Ramírez ·

Practigami

Vincent Achard - Ángel Ecija - Ilan Garibi - Sergio Guarachi - Larry Hart - Jens Kober - Ekaterina Lukasheva - Daniel Marchuk - Lily Marchuk - David Martínez - Tuấn Tú Nguyễn - snowblue - François Verdier - Graciela Vicente - Leire Vicente - Hubert Villeneuve - Atilla Yurtkul

NEORIGAMI

1.

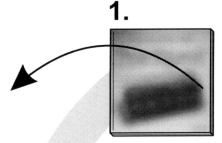

3.

2.

Contents

Step 1 3

Step 2: For going out 5

Monedero (Coin purse) 7

Purse 11

Step 3: For the yard 17

Etiquette de jardín (Garden labels) 19

Anemómetro (Anemometer) 21

Step 4: For playing around 25

Amarillas y rojas (Yellows and reds) 27

Flexi unit ball 33

Step 5: For the house 39

Phonestand 41

3D Portrait photo frame 43

Twister Lamp 48

Fuelle para chimenea (Fireplace bellows) 52

The nose 59

Step 6: For organizing & cleaning ----------------------------------- 73

Pockets for useful things ----------------------------------- 75

Dust pan ----------------------------------- 77

Garbage can ----------------------------------- 79

Grabber ----------------------------------- 89

Step 7: For dining ----------------------------------- 97

Vaso contenedor de agua (Water holding cup) ----------------------------------- 99

Bowl ----------------------------------- 101

Spoon ----------------------------------- 103

Condiment shakers ----------------------------------- 105

Rana mondadientes (Toothpick frog) ----------------------------------- 109

Step 8: For other reasons ----------------------------------- 121

Pointed square ----------------------------------- 123

Voodoo Doll ----------------------------------- 129

The finished model ----------------------------------- 135

Step 1

During March and part of April 2012 I (Gerardo) hosted the Inter-forum Useful Model Challenge in six different origami forums: Love Origami and Oriart (in Russian), Pajarita (in Spanish), PLIAGEDEPAPIER (in French), The Origami Forum (in English), and Vietnam Origami Group (in Vietnamese). The challenge was sponsored by Origami-shop.com and the collaborative blog Neorigami. Fellow origamist Aurèle Duda helped organizing the challenge in the French forum, Ekaterina Lukasheva in both Russian forums, and Hoàng Tiến Quyết in the Vietnamese one. 57 models were presented by 31 creators from all six forums. We had two winners; Atilla Yurtkul's *Condiment shakers* was chosen by the votes of fellow participants and Eric Strand's *Sleeve for CD/DVD & liner* was selected by the challenge's judges (Ángel Ecija from Spain, Larry Hart from England, and Didier Boursin from France).

With great joy I present to you the fruit of that challenge. Most of the models in here were created for the challenge, a couple are new models from the participants; the judges have also included original designs, as well as I. The following diagrams differ in styles, languages and complexity levels, yet they are all based in the traditional diagramming symbols; find information of each one in the web. For your convenience, the book is organized in different contexts of use: origami for...

I would like to thank J. Juan Campos, Jens Kober, and Graciela Vicente for their particular help in the development of this book: so sorry for all the hassle guys.

Step 2:

For going out

MONEDERO

David Martinez, 2012
Dibujos: Graciela Vicente
Papel elefante 20x20

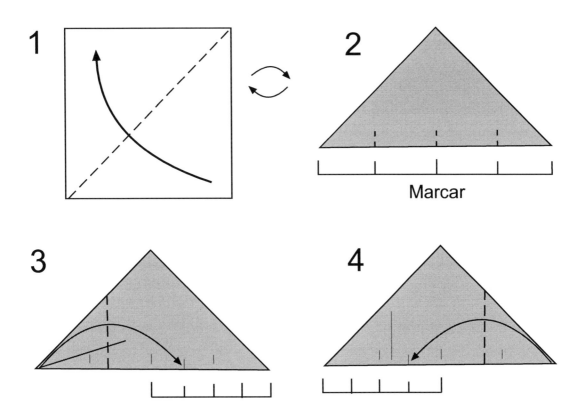

1

2

Marcar

3

4

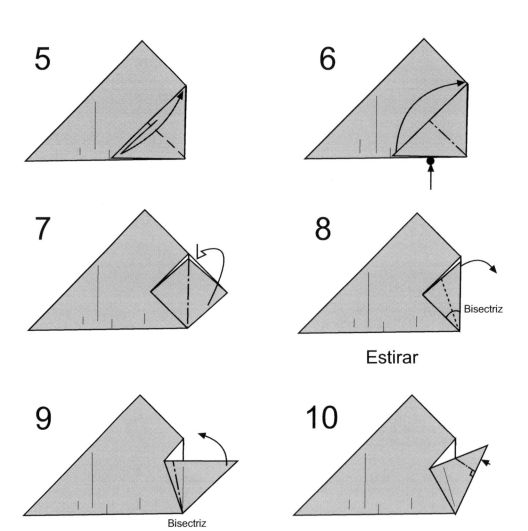

5

6

7

8

Bisectriz

Estirar

9

Bisectriz

10

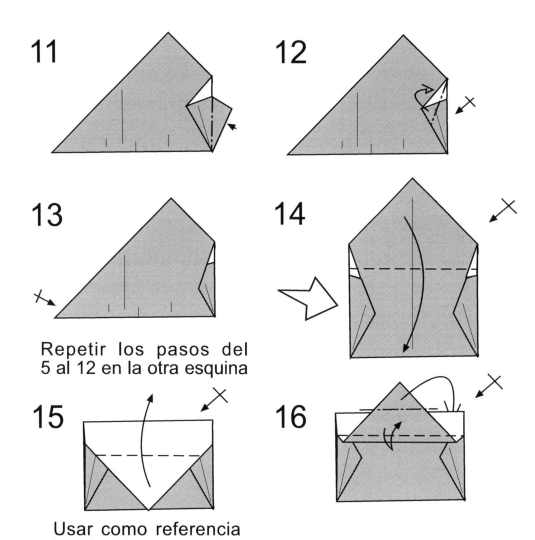

11

12

13

Repetir los pasos del
5 al 12 en la otra esquina

14

15

Usar como referencia
las cicatrices marcadas

16

17

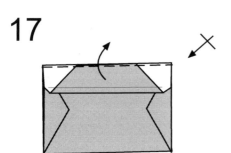

18

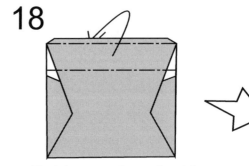

Doblar por las cicatrices premarcadas.

19

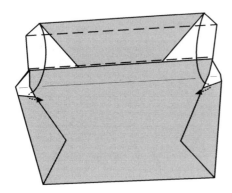

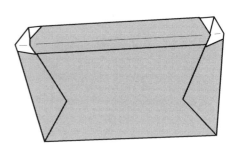

Modelo acabado.

Purse

by Daniel Marchuk (11 years old)
Diagrams: Juan Campos

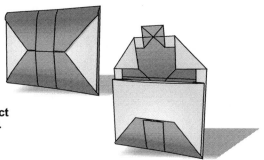

Two 25 X 25 cm. squares

Tear resistant sheets, like Tyvek or contact
paper, makes the purse last a lot longer.
Glue is optional.

First square

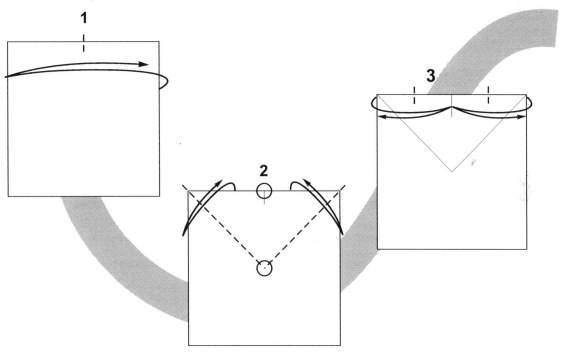

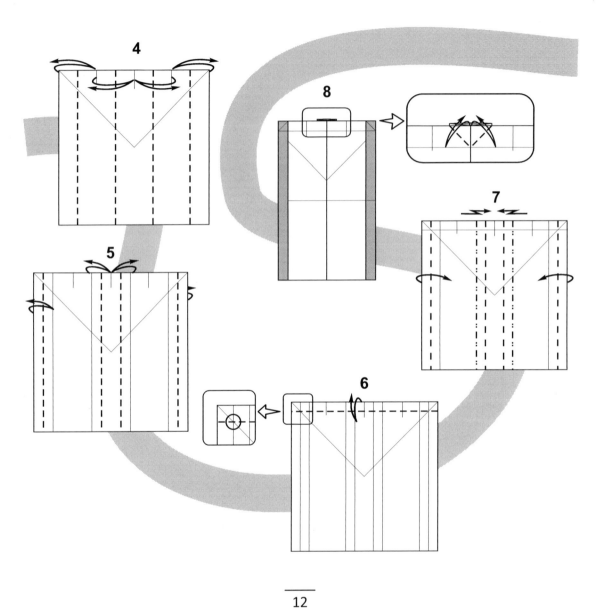

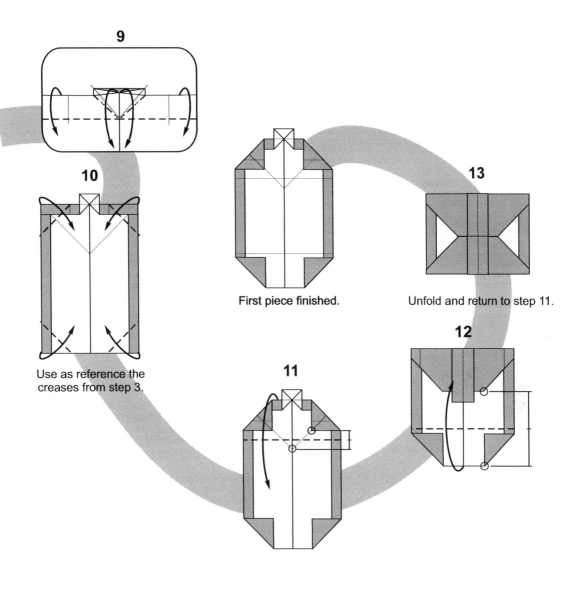

9

10

Use as reference the
creases from step 3.

First piece finished.

11

12

13

Unfold and return to step 11.

Second square

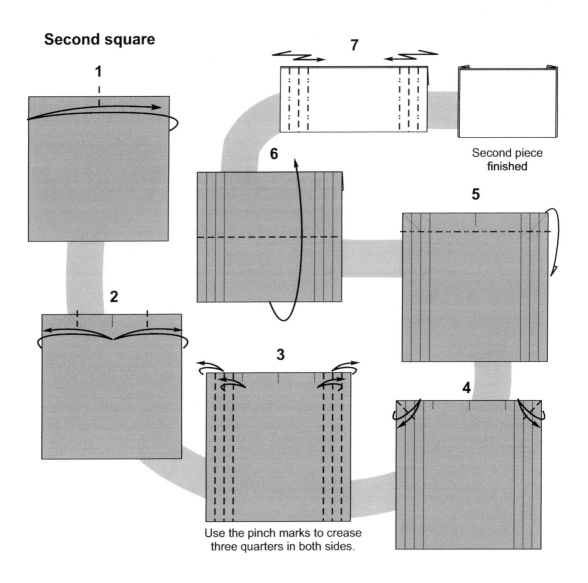

1

2

3

Use the pinch marks to crease
three quarters in both sides.

4

5

6

7

Second piece
finished

Assembly

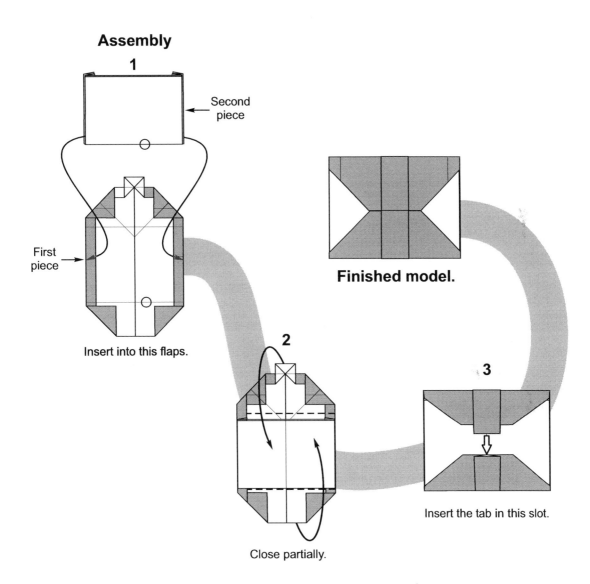

1

Second piece

First piece

Insert into this flaps.

Finished model.

2

Close partially.

3

Insert the tab in this slot.

Step 3:

For the yard

Etiquette de Jardin

François VERDIER c mars 2012

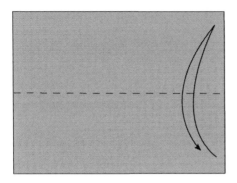

1- Partir d'une feuille de format A, l'étiquette aura la largeur du petit côté de la feuille et 4 cm de hauter pour une feuille A5. Plier et déplier selon la médiane.

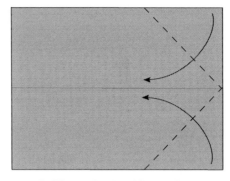

2- Plier selon les bissectrices

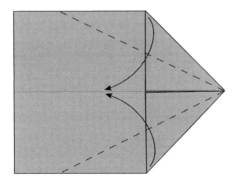

3- Plier selon les bissectrices

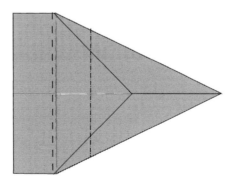

4- Plier en vallée puis en montagne

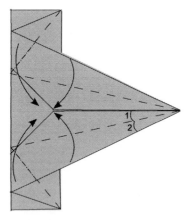

5- Pli pivot selon la bissectrice
de la grande pointe

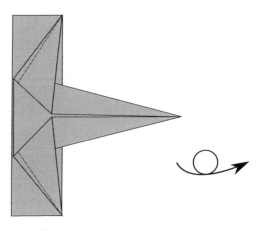

6- Tourner le modèle

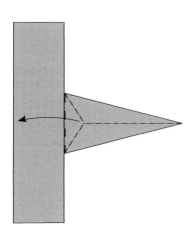

7- Oreille de lapin + un pli vallée

Tomate MARMANDE
Mai 2012

ANEMÓMETRO

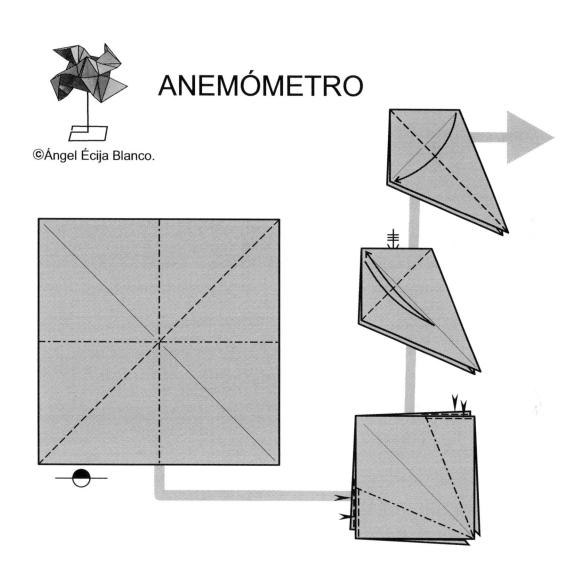

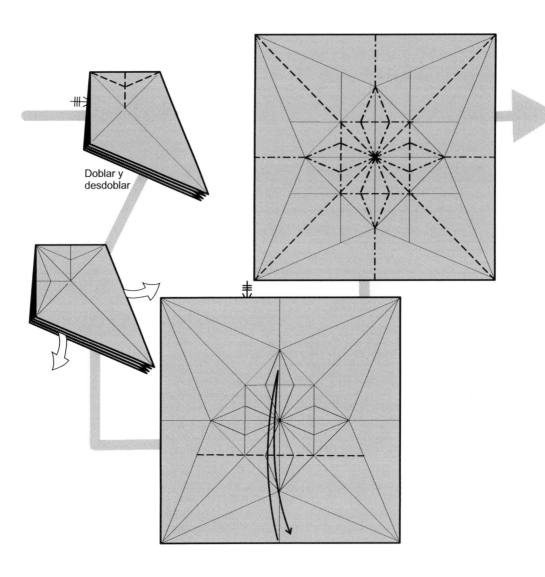

Doblar y
desdoblar

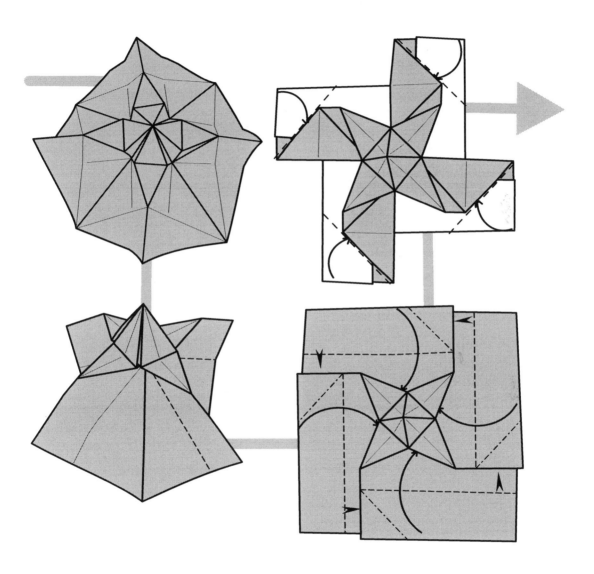

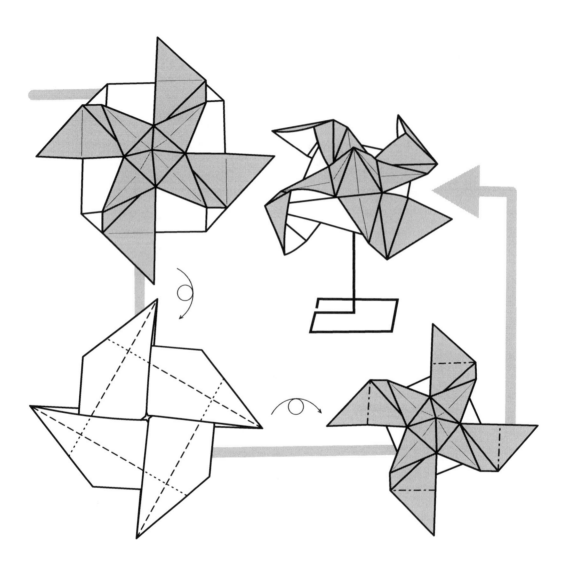

Step 4:

For playing around

AMARILLAS Y ROJAS

Graciela Vicente, 2012

☐ Color azul

▨ Color amarillo

■ Color rojo

MODULO A

Tamaño recomendado 10cmx10cm

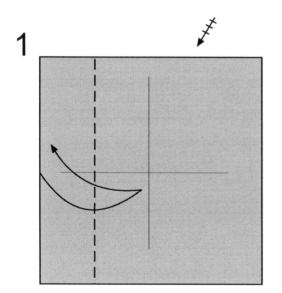

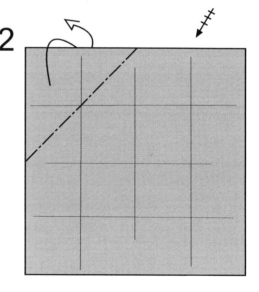

Marcar

3

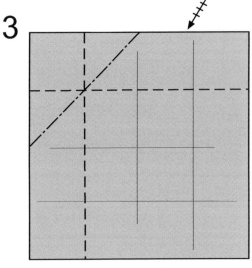

Realizar una base preliminar
en cada una de las puntas.

4

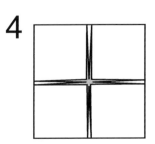

5

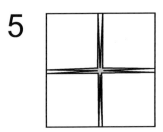

Realizar 12 módulos con el exterior
azul y el interior amarillo

6

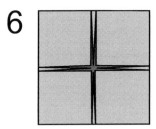

Realizar 12 módulos con el exterior
amarillo y el interior rojo.

MODULO B
Tamaño recomendado 5cmx5cm

1
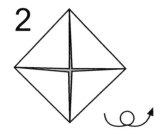

2
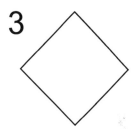

3

Realizar 17 módulos
azules

UNION DE LOS MODULOS

1 **2**
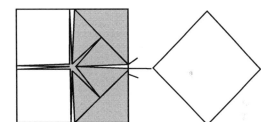

3
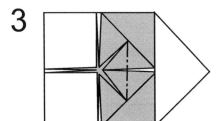

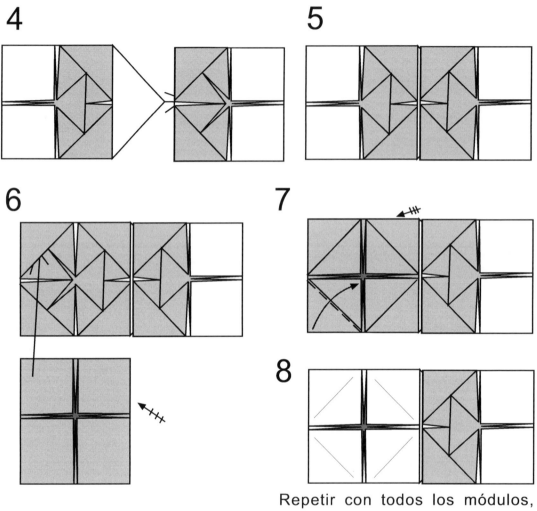

4

5

6

7

8

Repetir con todos los módulos,
haciendo una rejilla de 3x4 módulos.

TABLERO COMPLETO

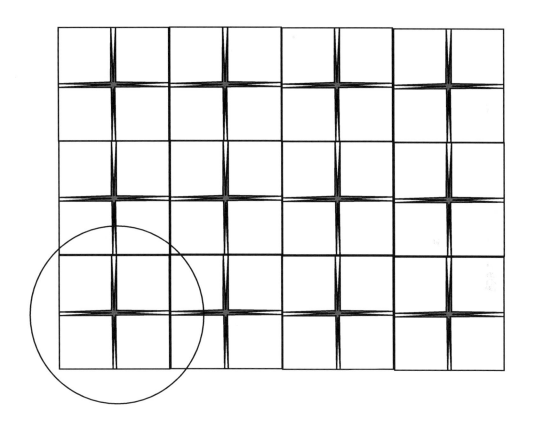

Vista en detalle

Movimiento ficha amarilla.

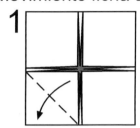 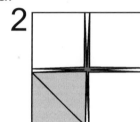

Movimiento ficha roja

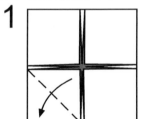 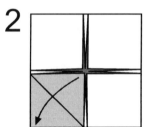 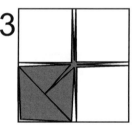

COMO JUGAR

Un jugador coloca las fichas amarillas y el otro las fichas rojas.
Sólo se puede colocar una ficha en la fila inferior o encima de
una ficha ya colocada.
Sólo se puede colocar una ficha por turno.
Gana aquel que haya colocado cuatro fichas del mismo
color en línea recta: horizontal, vertical o diagonal.

Flexi Unit Ball
Design and diagram by Ilan Garibi, 2011
30 units

This unit is flexible. So flexible, you can make a ball from it. The ball you get is stable, but to stand kicking and rough handling, I advice to glue the tabs in the pockets.

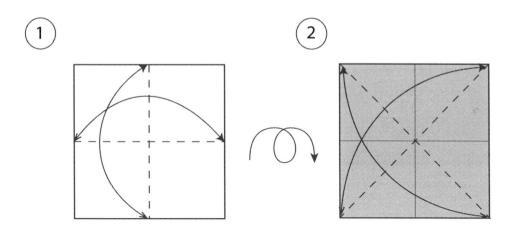

Start with the colour side down . Fold as marked, and unfold. Turn over.

Fold as marked, and unfold.

3

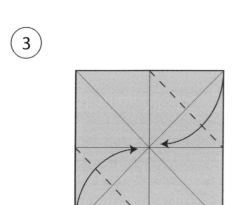

Valley fold two opposite corners to the centre.

4

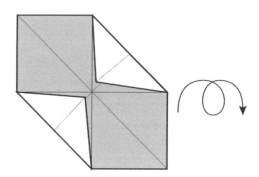

Turn over.

5

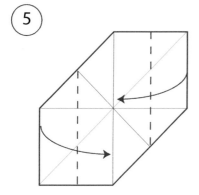

Valley fold right and left sides to the centre.

6

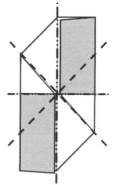

Make a preliminary base .

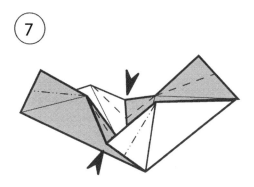

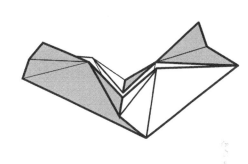

Fold the tabs as shown. Note the left is mountain fold while the right is valley. Then inside reverse fold the corners.

This is the final unit, but for easy assembly you should unfold the tabs, and the reverse folds of the pockets.

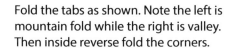

Assembly:

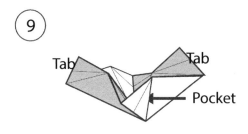

Tab   Tab

Pocket

The final unit, after unfolding steps 7-8.

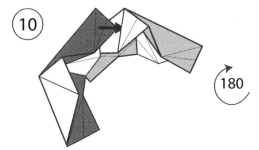

180

Insert a Tab into the next unit`s Pocket.

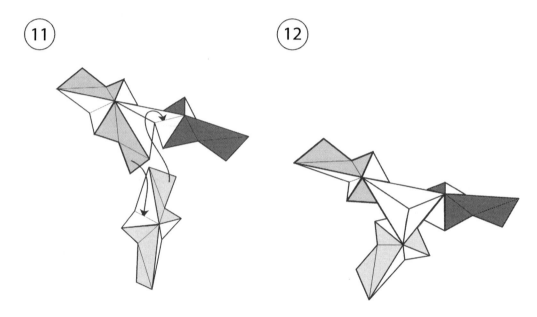

(11)

This view is rotated. Insert third unit Tab into the first unit's pocket, while closing the triangle by inserting second unit tab into the third unit's pocket

(12)

Three units assembled.

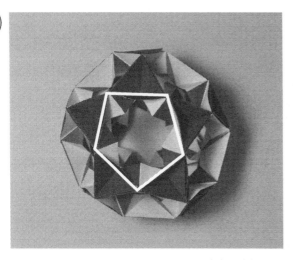

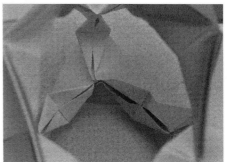

Three units locked together (a view from the inside of the ball).

To get the ball, connect all 30 units. While adding new units, make a pentagon surrounded by triangles. Note that the first pentagon with all triangles asks for ten units! Keep on adding units at the same pattern.

When completed, the ball should have 12 pentagons.

Your ball is ready!

Step 5:

For the house

Phone Stand
created by snowblue

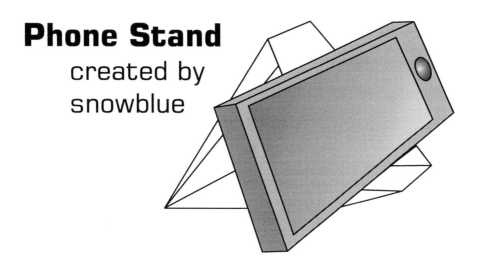

1.

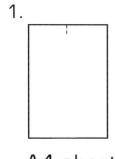

A4 sheet

2.

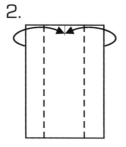

3.

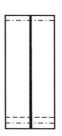

Each
segment
has 1 cm.

4.

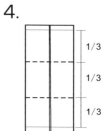

1/3

1/3

1/3

5.

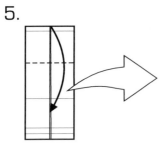

6.

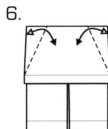

7.

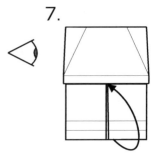

Insert the bottom
inside the slot

8.

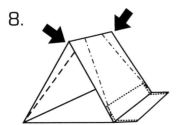

9.

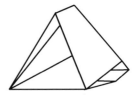

The phone
stand is ready

3D Portrait Photo-Frame

Model: Larry Hart
Diagrams: Jens Kober

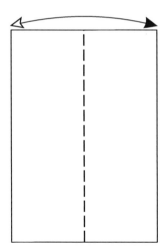

1. Start with A4 or similar. Fold and unfold vertically in half.

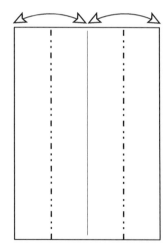

2. Fold and unfold.

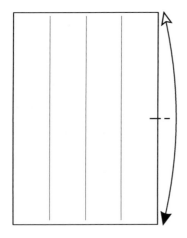

3. Pinch fold 1/2.

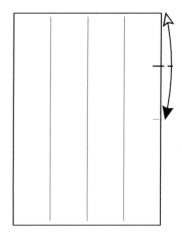

4. Pinch fold 1/4.

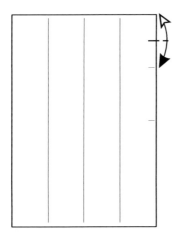

5. Pinch fold 1/8.

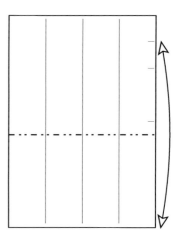

6. Fold bottom edge to 1/8 and unfold.

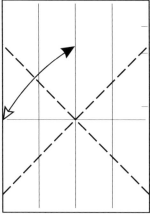

7. Fold and unfold.

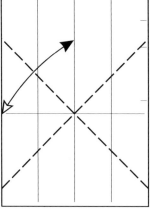

8. Collapse waterbomb base.

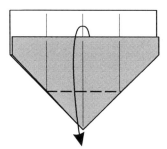

9. Open the first layer...

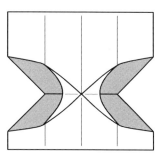

10. ... and squash.

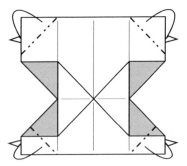

11. Fold the corners behind.

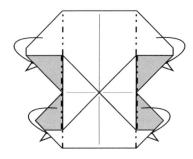

12. Fold the sides behind.

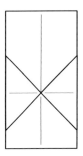

13. Place the photo in the center.

14. Fold the top and bottom along the edge of the photo.

15. Insert each corner of the photo inside the pockets.

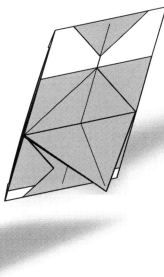

Twister lamp

© Lukasheva Ekaterina, 2011

For this model use 30 pieces of paper with the ratio 1:2. If you use the paper of the size
a x 2a, the resulting sphere will be around 2a in diameter. Use folder or other comfortable device to make the creases precise and well folded.

Choose the paper size to make the model big enough to contain the lamp and the lamp holder. The lamp should not touch the paper. Choose power-saving, diode or other low temperature lamps. Hot lamps placed in paper lampshades can cause fire. Don't leave the lit lamp unattended.

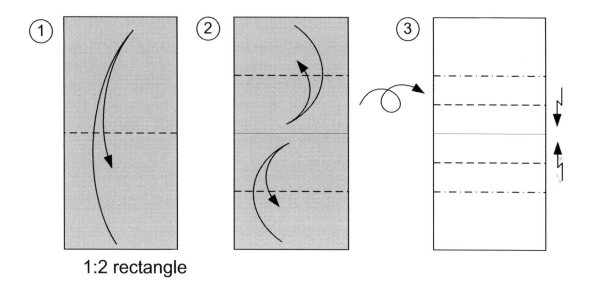

1:2 rectangle

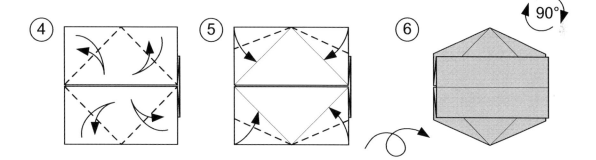

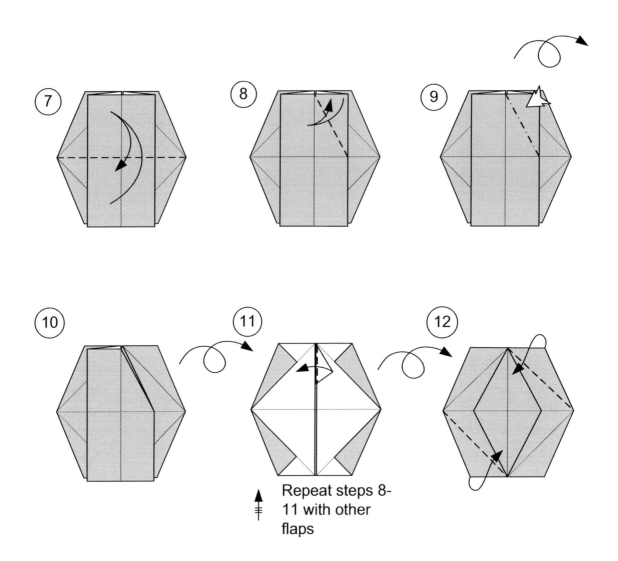

Repeat steps 8-
11 with other
flaps

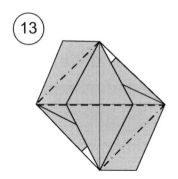

(13)

Reinforce the shown creases
The unit is complete

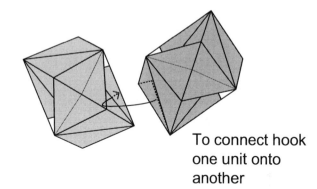

To connect hook one unit onto another

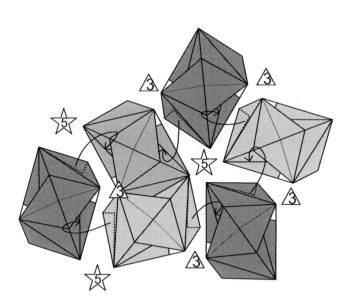

You need 30 units for a complete ball. Connect units to triangular pyramids (each triangle marks the vertex of the pyramid). Assembled pyramid becomes stable. Five pyramids should touch in the places marked with a star.

While assembling the last units pass the lamp holder into the ball. Let the cord pass through the vertex of the pyramid. Since the vertex is a bit flexible, it won't be a problem.

Fuelle para Chimenea

Modelo: *Gerardo Gacharná*
Diagramas: *Alexander Oliveros*
y un colaborador anónimo

Consigue dos pliegos (70 X 100 cm) de cartulina oscura del mismo color y dos pliegos de papel kraft de color café. Corta y pega juntos los cuatro pliegos para crear un rectángulo bicolor de 68 X 170 cm. Para mejorar la efectividad del fuelle necesitarás además cinta adhesiva de embalaje, un par de tablas de tríplex (contrachapado) y plastilina limpiatipos, también conocida como Blu-Tack. Mira el paso 16 para tener una idea del tamaño de las tablas de tríplex).

Para practicar con una hoja más pequeña, usa un rectángulo de papel regalo de 20 X 50 cm. Puedes usar cinta de la más angosta y tablitas de Fórmica o cartón paja, junto con la plastilina limpiatipos, para que funcione mejor.

Encuentra detalles, imágenes y un video del *Fuelle para chimenea* acá:
http://www.neorigami.com/neo/index.php/es/modelos-utiles/item/366-fuelle-para-chimenea-/-fireplace-bellows

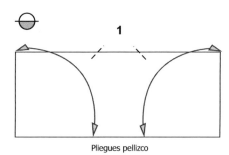

Pliegues pellizco

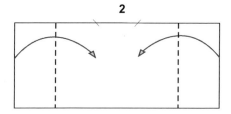

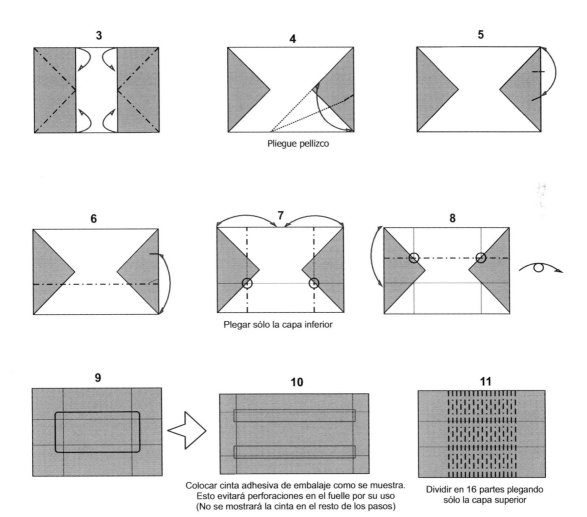

3

4

Pliegue pellizco

5

6

7

Plegar sólo la capa inferior

8

9

10

Colocar cinta adhesiva de embalaje como se muestra.
Esto evitará perforaciones en el fuelle por su uso
(No se mostrará la cinta en el resto de los pasos)

11

Dividir en 16 partes plegando
sólo la capa superior

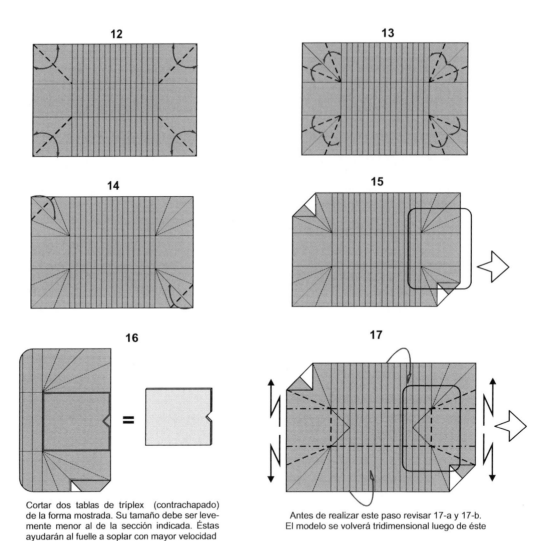

12

13

14

15

16

Cortar dos tablas de tríplex (contrachapado) de la forma mostrada. Su tamaño debe ser levemente menor al de la sección indicada. Éstas ayudarán al fuelle a soplar con mayor velocidad

17

Antes de realizar este paso revisar 17-a y 17-b. El modelo se volverá tridimensional luego de éste

17-a

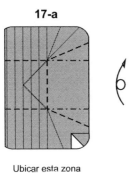

Ubicar esta zona

17-b

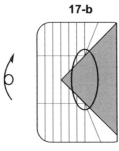

Al plegar el paso 17, NO plegar la punta mostrada

18

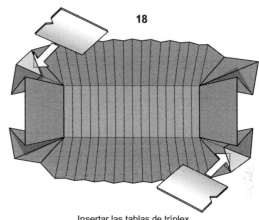

Insertar las tablas de tríplex (contrachapado) como se indica

19

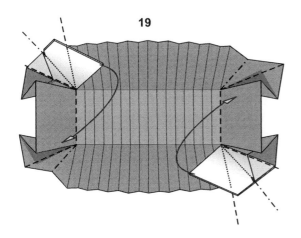

20

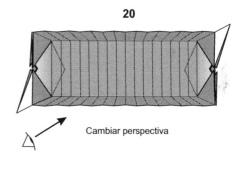

Cambiar perspectiva

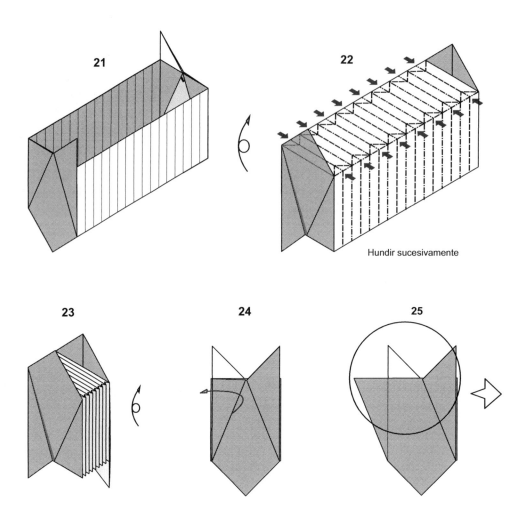

21

22

Hundir sucesivamente

23

24

25

26

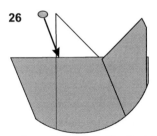

Acomodar una bolita de plastilina limpiatipos
(Blu-Tack) encima de las capas acumuladas.
La plastilina tapará los escapes de aire.

27

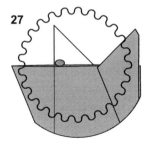

Vista entrecortada en
la parte indicada.

28

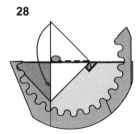

29

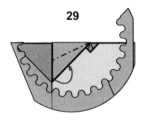

30

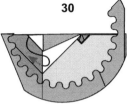

Insertar la punta en el bolsillo

31

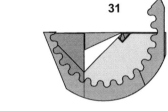

32

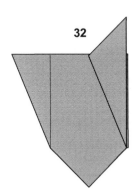

33

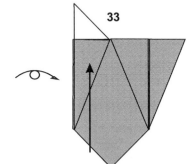

Repetir pasos 24-30

34

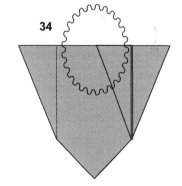

35

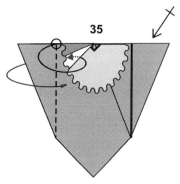

Insertar el punto indicado en el bolsillo
en ambos lados y al mismo tiempo

36

Modelo terminado

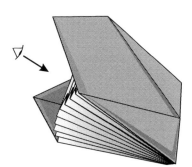

Manera de utilizarlo

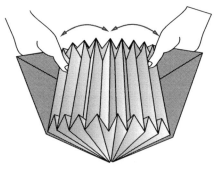

Para usarlo, ubicar los dedos gordos
en el primer y último segmento del acordeón

The Nose

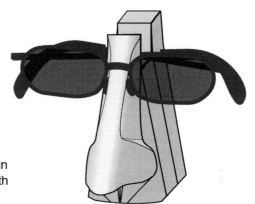

Model & Diagram
Jens Kober, 2012

An A4 sized paper works well with real glasses. You can fold the model with plain (copy) paper but backing it with foil will help with the final shaping.

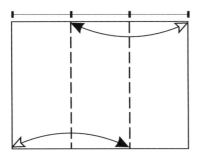

1. Start with the inside side up. Divide the long side into thirds.

2. Mark the center of the short side with a pinch. Then pinch at 1/4.

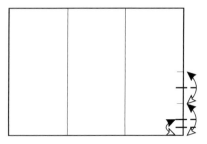

3. Mark 1/8, 3/8, and 1/16.

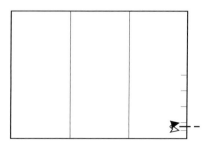

4. Finally mark 3/32.

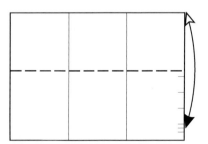

5. Fold the far long edge to the 3/32 mark.

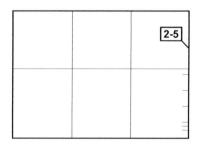

6. Repeat steps 2-5 on the upper side or simply fold the edge in half and transfer the marks needed in step 5 and 7.

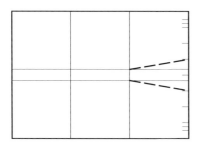

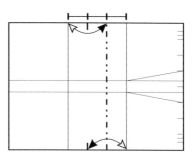

7. Add two valley folds starting a the 3/8 and 5/8 marks. This is going to be the back of the model.

8. Divide the center part into thirds. Mountain fold the right third, only pinch the left one.

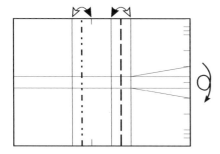

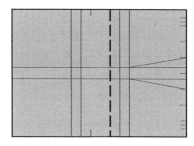

9. Using the creases of the previous step, add a mountain and a valley fold. Turn over.

10. Valley fold on the existing line.

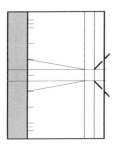

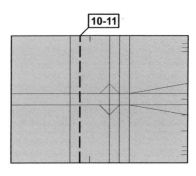

11. Add two 45° creases through both layers. Unfold to step 10.

12. Repeat step 10 and 11 on the indicated line.

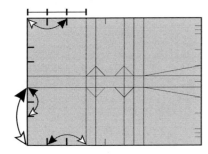

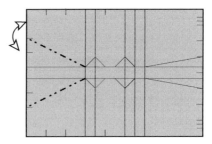

13. Result of step 12. Mark 1/3 and 2/3 on the top and bottom as well as 1/2 and 3/4 on the sides.

14. Add two mountain folds between the pinch marks and the intersection of the indicated creases.

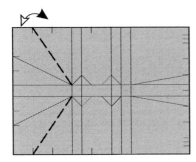

15. Add two valley folds between the pinch marks and the same intersection.

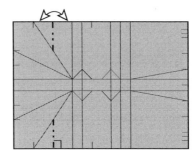

16. Add two mountain folds starting at the indicated pinch marks. The creases should be perpendicular to the edge. Stop when they hit the creases from step 15.

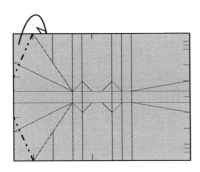

17. Fold the two edges behind. The fold is between the two pinches shown. The pinches will not be shown from now on.

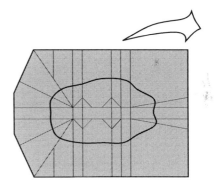

18. Result of step 12. Enlarged view.

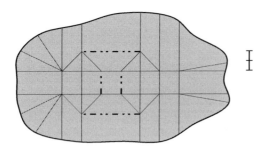

19. Add mountain folds where indicated.

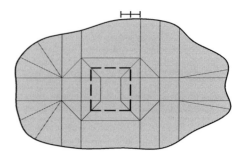

20. Add valley folds that run between the parallel creases on view. Ready to collapse...

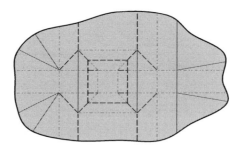

21. Make sure all creases are in the indicated direction, you will have to reverse a few. The next steps will illustrate the collapse process.

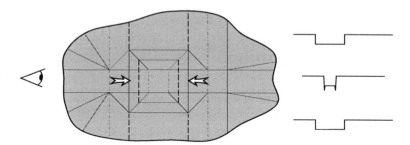

22. Fold the indicated creases. From the underside, push towards the center where shown. Seen from the side, the paper should get the profiles on view. The next view is from above the paper towards the back of the model.

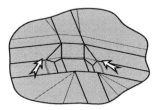

23. Pop the gray creases up and push the corners in. The remainder of the creases should collapse almost automatically.

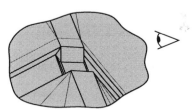

24. In progress. Swing the sides down to get 90° angles on top. Next view from the side.

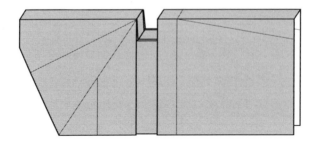

25. Collapse process done.

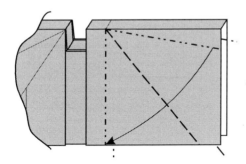

26. Change these two existing creases to mountain folds. Valley fold to make them line up. Straighten the back. Repeat behind.

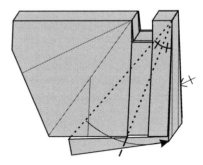

27. Valley fold the flaps you just created on their angle bisectors. The edge lines up with the corner of the model.

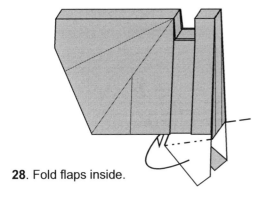

28. Fold flaps inside.

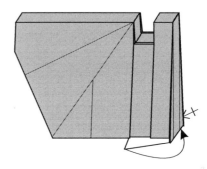

29. Swing the two flaps to the backside of the model.

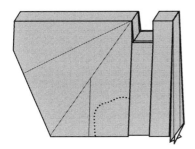

30. Cutaway view.

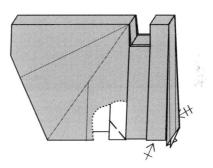

31. Fold both layers together. They will be tucked under the top layer. Repeat on the three other pleats.

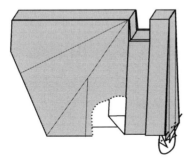

32. On the back, fold all excess paper into the model.

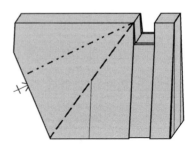

33. Reform the creases from steps 14 & 15 on both sides. Allow the nasal bridge to bend.

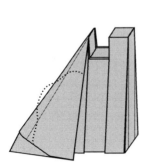

34. The next view cuts away the top layer. Slightly enlarged view.

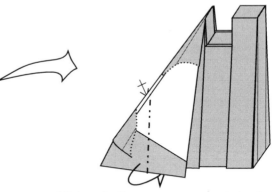

35. Locate the crease you made in step 16 and fold the complete flap inside the model. Repeat behind.

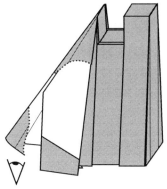

36. Next view from below.

37. Press the two flaps you just folded behind together and make their front edges line up. The paper below the nose will bend.

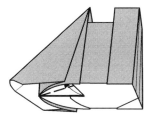

38. Fold these two flaps together.

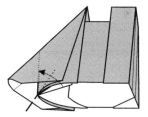

39. Fold them together once more in the same direction to lock the front of the model.

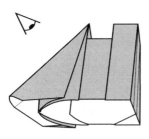

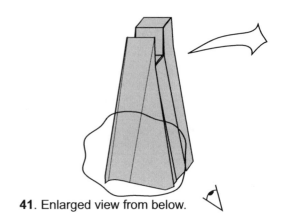

40. The next view is from the front.

41. Enlarged view from below.

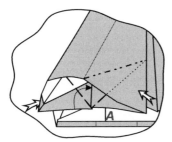

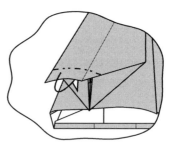

42. Inside reverse fold the corners of the nose. Point **A** ends up inside the nose on the center line.

43. Fold the tip of the nose behind.

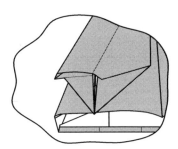

44. Back to the view from step 41. The next steps are shaping folds, so don't make the creases sharp.

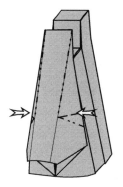

45. Push the sides of the nose in. The vertical mountain folds already exist. The others don't have any references. Allow the base behind the nose to curve.

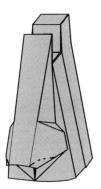

46. Round the nose where the nostrils would be.

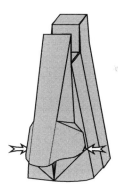

47. Push in the corners.

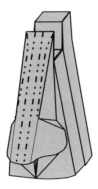

48. Round the nasal bridge and adjust it so your glasses fit.

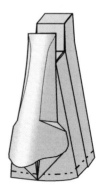

49. Mountain fold around the whole bottom edge of the model to lock it.

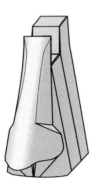

50. Generally round the nose. Shape until you are happy (a mirror might be helpful)

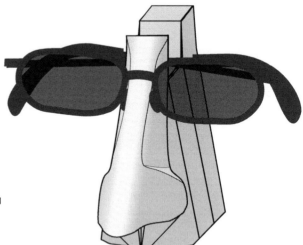

Step 6:

For organizing and cleaning

Pockets for Useful Things
by Lily Marchuk

Diagrams: Lily Marchuk & Juan Campos

Start with a big and strong
paper of 1.5 X 1 proportions,
like 60 X 40 cm cardstock

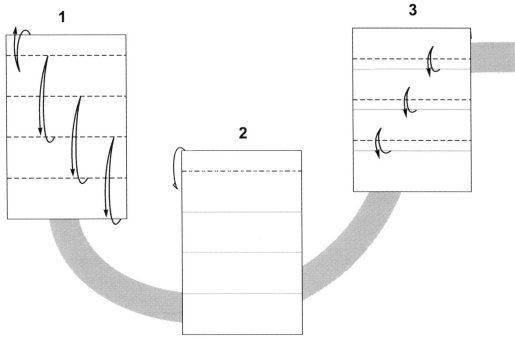

1

2

3

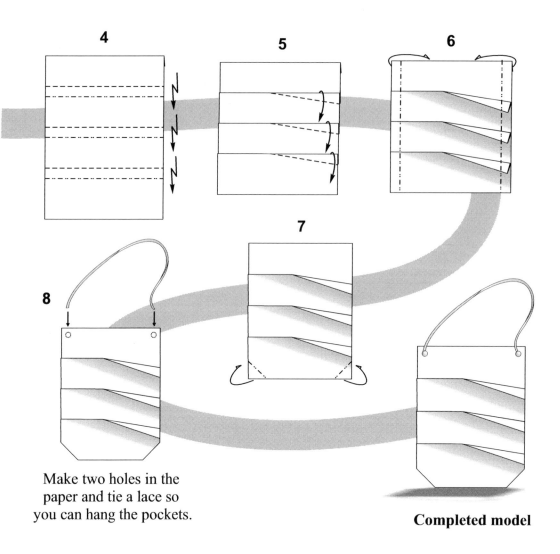

4

5

6

7

8

Make two holes in the
paper and tie a lace so
you can hang the pockets.

Completed model

Dust pan

Creator: Nguyen Tu Tuan (VOG)
Designed: 04/2012
Paper size: 10x20 cm

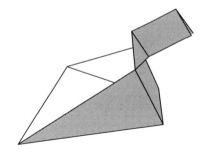

1

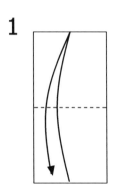

Fold and unfold

2

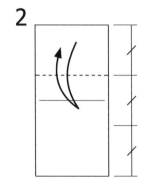

Pre-crease

3

Pre-crease

4

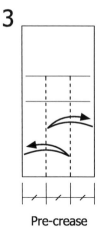

Pre-crease

5

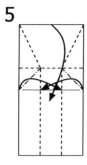

Fold as crease

6

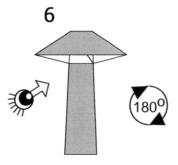

Look at this direction.

180°

7

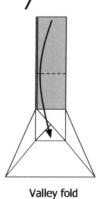

Valley fold

8

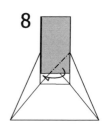

Mountain fold, hide the upper layer inside.

9

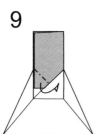

Mountain fold
and hide below
the second layer

10

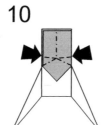

Push paper in, at both side.

11

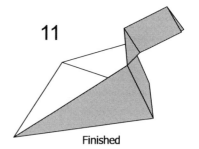

Finished

Garbage Can
Design and diagram by Ilan Garibi, 2012
www.garibiorigami.com
garibiilan@gmail.com

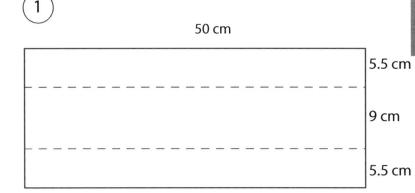

(1)

50 cm

5.5 cm

9 cm

5.5 cm

Final size is:
Height: ~12 cm
Length: ~10 cm
Width: ~ 9 cm

Start with a rectangle, 20x50 cm. Measure and fold as marked, to get an overlapping flaps in the centre.

(2)

To get this.

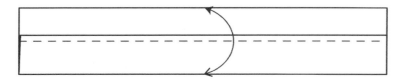

Fold and unfold in half

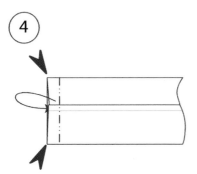

We start with the bin on the left side.
Sink in 2 cm to lock all layers together.

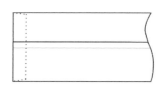

To this position.

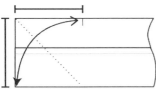

Mark a the width of the strip on the length with a pinch.

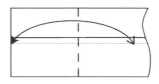

Continue the pinch with a valley fold.

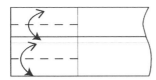

Fold and unfold edges to the centre, stop the fold lines just before the vertical fold line.

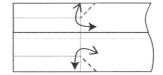

Add two diagonal valley folds, by bringing top and bottom edges to the vertical crease line. Crease only until the horizontal crease line.

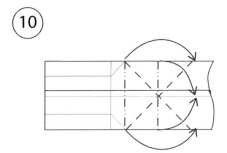

(10)

Add two valley folds and a
mountain fold and make a Water
Bomb base on the right side of
the vertical fold line.

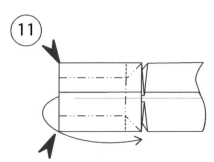

(11)

Create the bin by squashing the
upper and lower edges, along the
marked mountain folds, and rotate
the left side to point upward.

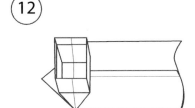

(12)

To get this.

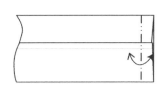

(13)

Now we fold the lid.
Fold 1 cm width strip with a
mountain fold and unfold.

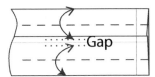

Valley fold edges to a gap of 3 mm from both sides of the centre line, and unfold. This gap will ensure the lid is wider than the bin. The length of the fold line is about 15 cm.

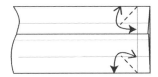

Add two diagonal valley folds, by bringing top and bottom edges to the vertical crease line. Crease to the point where each one meets the corresponding crease lines.

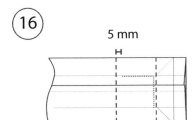

5 mm

Fold the right valley fold at the junctions with the diagonal folds. Unfold.
The reference to the left fold is equal to the width (marked with a dotted line) plus 5 mm, starting from the right valley fold you just made. Unfold.

Add two diagonal valley folds, by bringing top and bottom edges to the left most vertical crease line. Crease to the point where each one meets the corresponding crease lines.

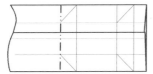

Add a mountain fold at the edge of the diagonal crease lines. Unfold.

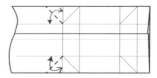

Add two more diagonal lines. Unfold.

20

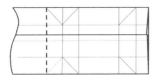

Add a valley fold at the left edge of the diagonal crease lines. Unfold.

21

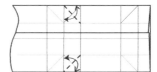

Add two more diagonal lines, crossing the second left diagonal lines. Unfold.

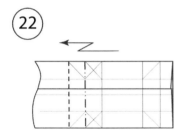

Start to shape the lid by pleating as marked (use existing creases only).

Go 3D now, by raising the left and right edges, as well as top and bottom.

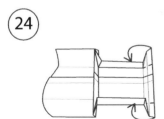

Fold the two flaps to the sides of the lid.

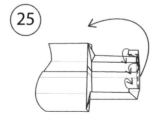

Tuck the 1 cm edge to lock the right side of the lid, and make the lid stand up.

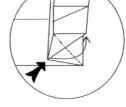

The lid is vertical here.
The following step is an enlarged
image of the marked area.

Inside reverse fold the corner.

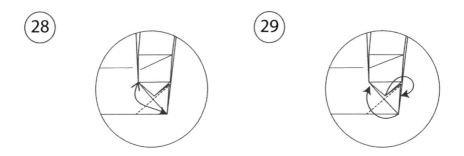

Fold and unfold the corner

Now fold again, but this time tuck the
small triangle flap into the pocket
that comes with the folded corner.
This will strengthen the lock (thanks
to Gerardo G. for that improvement)

(30)

Back to normal view. Repeat steps 27-29 in the other corner.

(31)

The lid is ready.

(32)

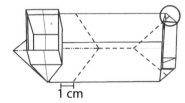

1 cm

Add the last needed valley folds. The right valley fold is slanted at around 45 degrees, dividing the marked little triangle.

On the left side start the fold line 1 cm from the edge of the bin. Do not crease strongly until you manage to locate the lid on top of the bin. Some adjustments are needed.

Those lines make a stiffer back that can transfer the movement of the front paddle to open and close the lid.

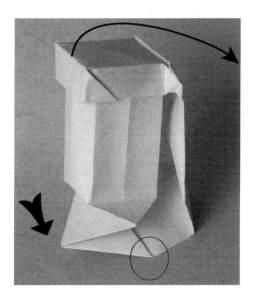 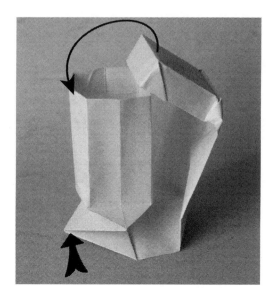

Hold the marked edge and the same on the other side between thumb and finger of your right hand. With the left hand pinch the pedal. By moving it downward, the lid will open. Moving it up will close it.

Grabber

Model: Gerardo Gacharná
Diagrams: Juan David Bernal
& Polo Madueño

You'll need poster board, plywood boards, and duct tape. Cut a 70 X 100cm poster board by its longer half and tape two ends together in order to get a 35 X 200 cm rectangle.   Also, look at step 20 to see the size of the plywood boards. You have to use a very strong tape so the boards won't shift as you use it; that's why you should use duct tape.

To practice with a smaller paper use a 10 X 55 cm paper rectangle and use Formica laminate instead of plywood. You'll still need duct tape.

Find details, pictures, and a video of the Grabber here:
**http://www.neorigami.com/neo/index.php/en/useful
-models/item/386-agarrador-/-grabber**

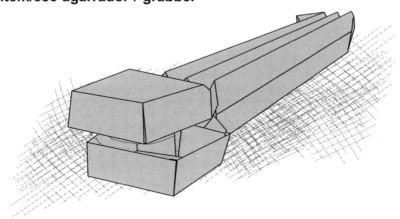

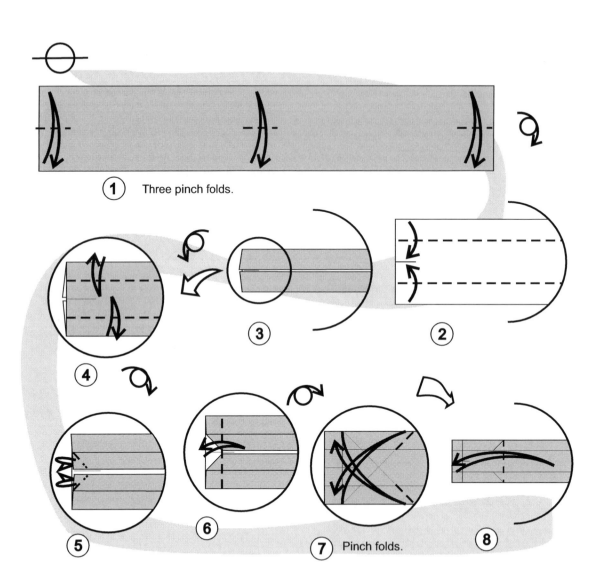

1. Three pinch folds.

2.

3.

4.

5.

6.

7. Pinch folds.

8.

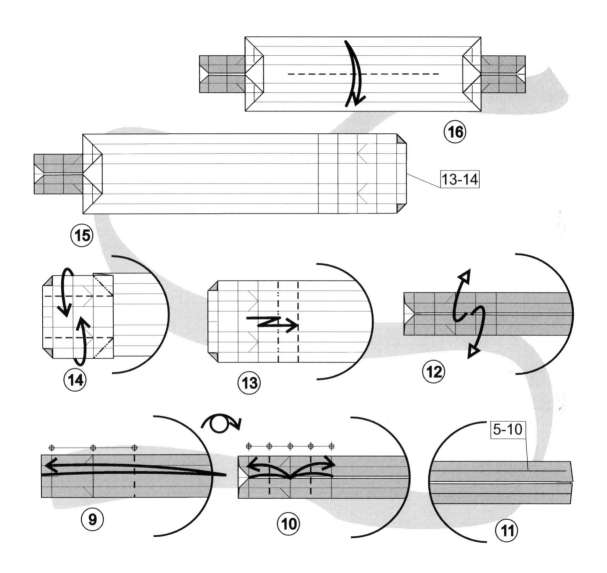

⑯

13-14

⑮

⑭ ⑬ ⑫

⑨ ⑩ 5-10 ⑪

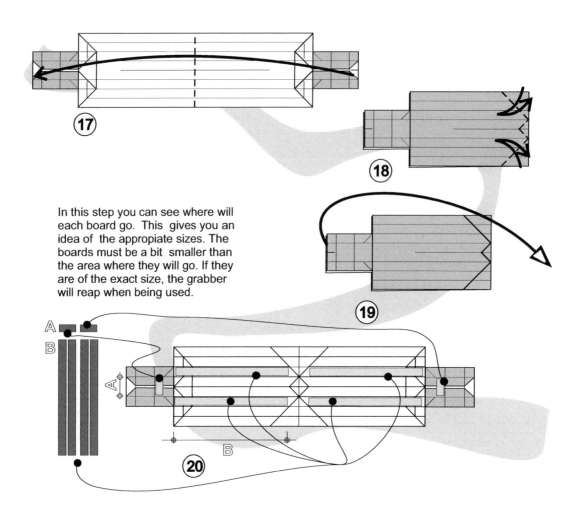

In this step you can see where will each board go. This gives you an idea of the appropiate sizes. The boards must be a bit smaller than the area where they will go. If they are of the exact size, the grabber will reap when being used.

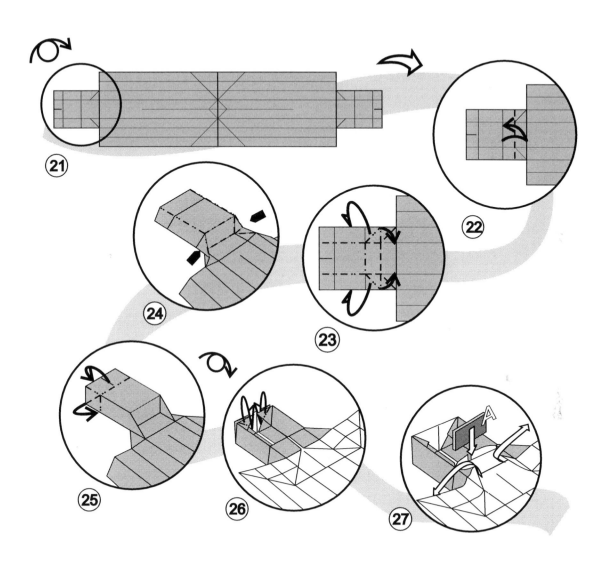

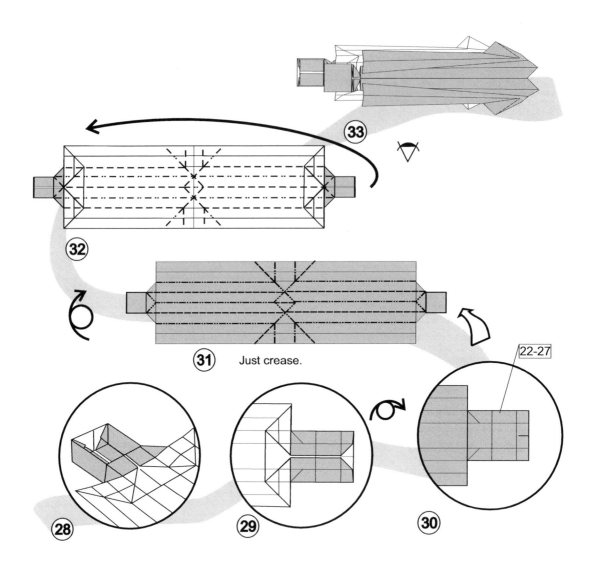

(31) Just crease.

22-27

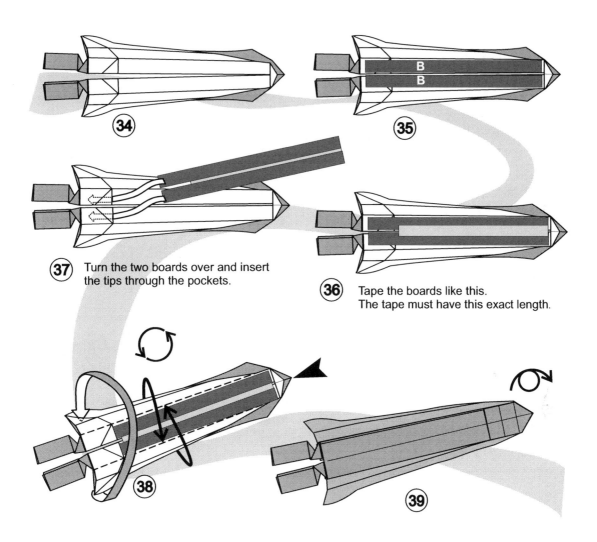

34

35

B
B

37 Turn the two boards over and insert the tips through the pockets.

36 Tape the boards like this.
The tape must have this exact length.

38

39

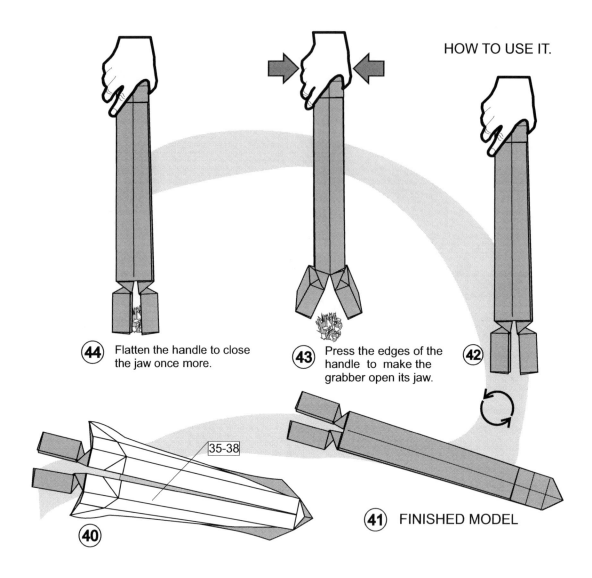

44 Flatten the handle to close the jaw once more.

43 Press the edges of the handle to make the grabber open its jaw.

42

41 FINISHED MODEL

40

35-38

Step 7:

For dining

VASO CONTENEDOR DE AGUA

Leire Vicente, 2012 (5 años de edad)

15x15

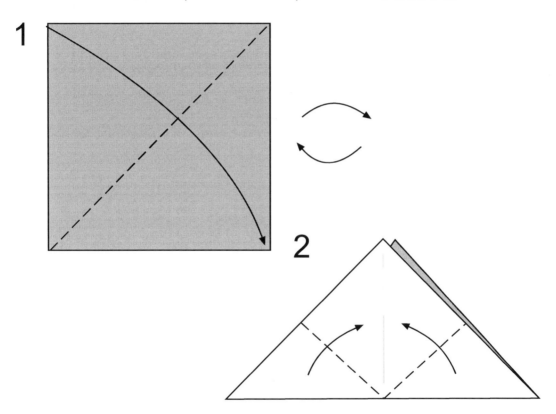

3

4

5

Abrir la figura

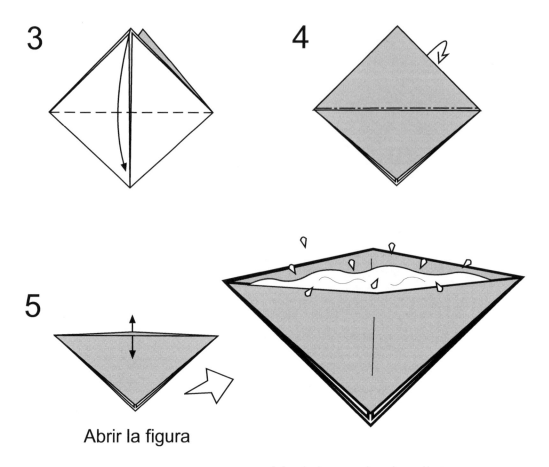

Modelo acabado; ¡listo para
llenarlo de agua!

BOWL

Creator: Nguyen Tu Tuan
Designed: 04/2012
Paper size: 15 x 15 cm.
Recommended material: silver or aluminium foil.

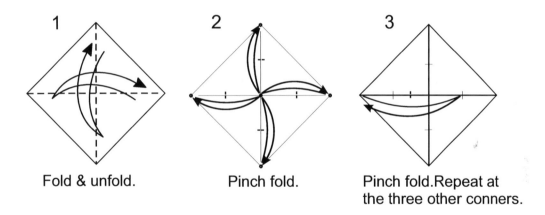

1
Fold & unfold.

2
Pinch fold.

3
Pinch fold.Repeat at
the three other conners.

4

Fold and unfold.

5

Radial pleat fold.

6

Mountain fold.

7

Valley fold. Repeat at the three other conners.

8

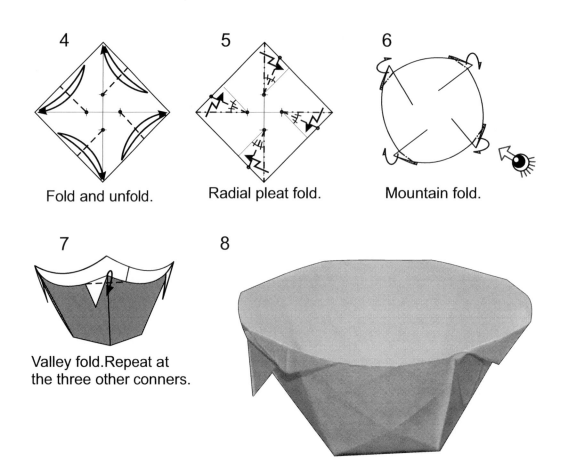

Finished.

SPOON

Creator: Nguyen Tu Tuan
Designed: 04/2012
Paper size: 10 x 20 cm.
Recommended material: silver or aluminium foil

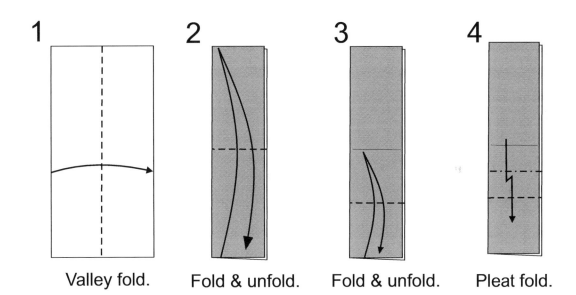

1   Valley fold.

2   Fold & unfold.

3   Fold & unfold.

4   Pleat fold.

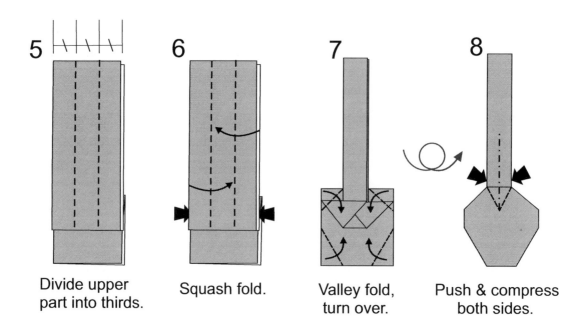

5 Divide upper part into thirds.

6 Squash fold.

7 Valley fold, turn over.

8 Push & compress both sides.

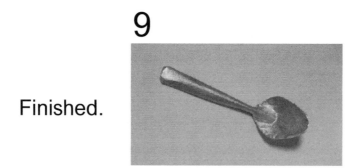

9 Finished.

CONDIMENT SHAKERS

Creator: Atilla YURTKUL
Diagramer: Kunsulu JILKISHIYEVA

Crease pattern (CP) on the last page of this diagrams.
Carefully transfer it to your paper. Recommended paper size: 21 X 21 cm
This line indicates the hole for big sized species such as thyme or red pepper.

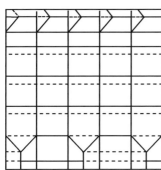

1. Crease according to the CP.
The solid lines represent mountain folds

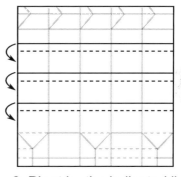

2. Pleat by the indicated lines

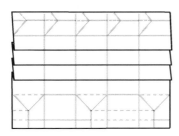

3.   ...like this...

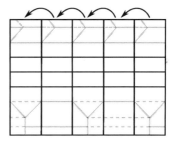

4. Now fold the vertical lines...

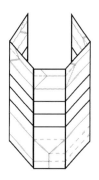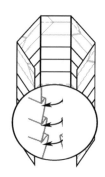

5. ... to make the 3D box base for the shaker

6. Connect the pleats by inserting one pleat inside the other

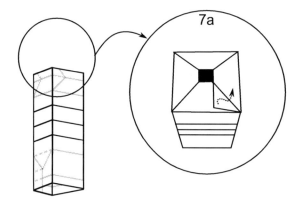

7a

7. Let's concentrate on the top.
   Fold following the creases
7a. Insert the little triangle into the pocket

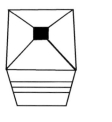

8. ... like this...

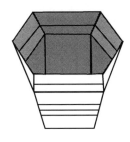

9. Close the bottom of the shaker

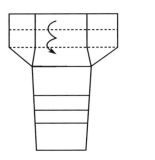

10. Fold the two layers together.

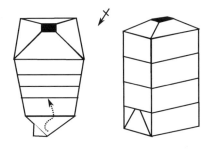

11. Insert the tips of the flaps
into the pockets

12. Thats all! Enjoy your meal!

"Rana - Mondadientes"

Sergio L. Guarachi V.
2012
La Paz - Bolivia

Papel Recomedado: 22x22 cm: Bicolor

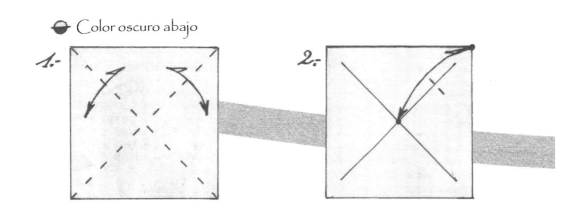

Color oscuro abajo

1.-

2.-

Sergio L. Guarachi V.

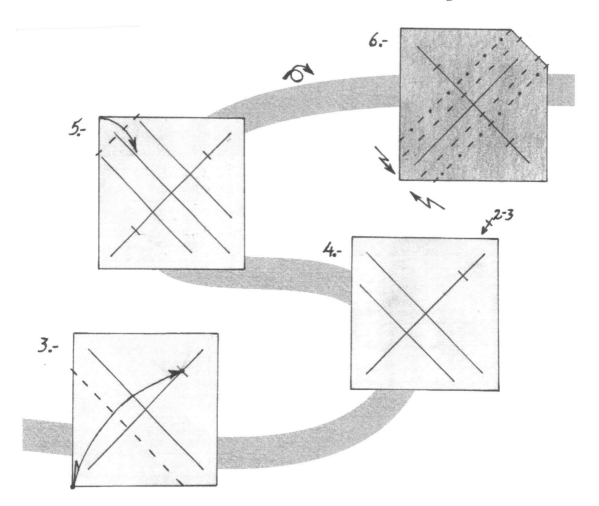

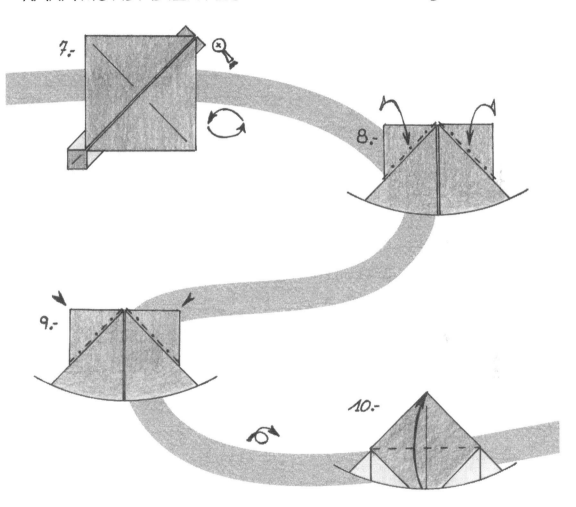

Sergio L. Guarachi V.

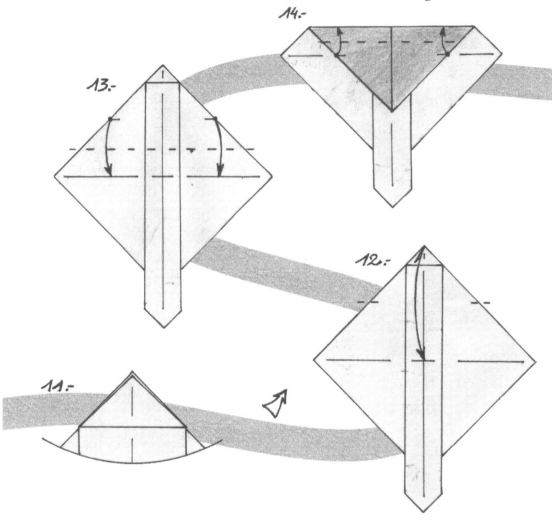

Sergio L. Guarachi V.

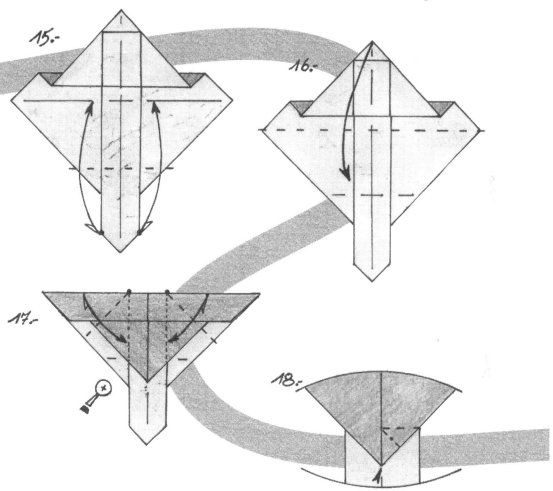

"RANA-MONDADIENTES"

Sergio L. Guarachi V.

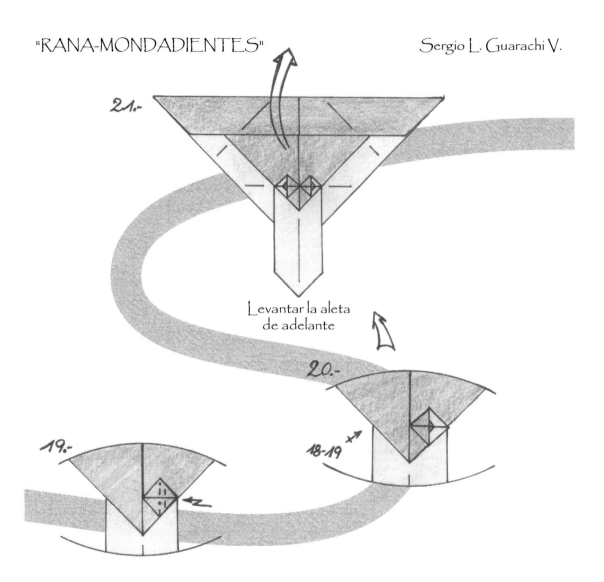

Levantar la aleta
de adelante

114

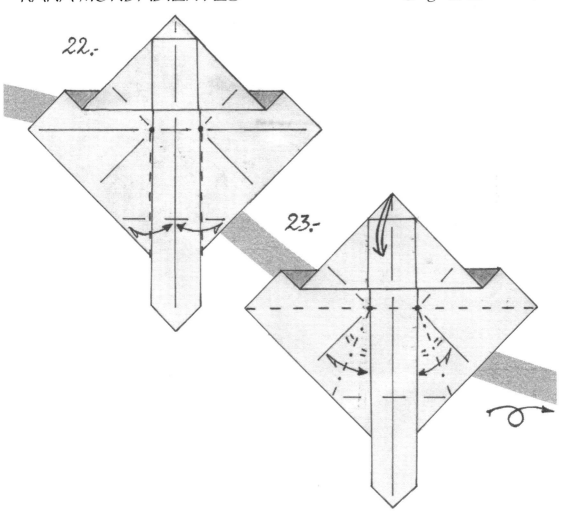

22.-

23.-

"RANA-MONDADIENTES"

Sergio L. Guarachi V.

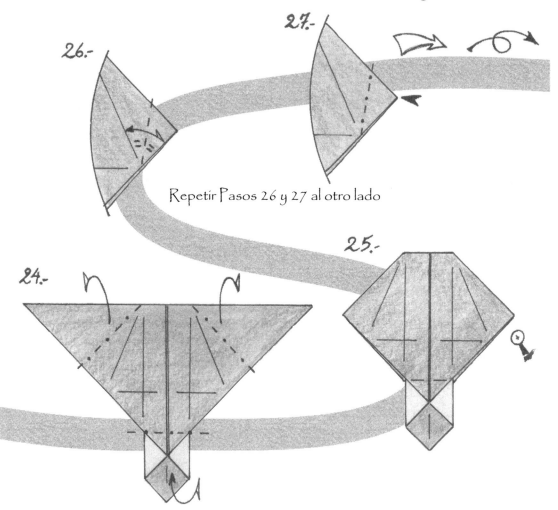

Repetir Pasos 26 y 27 al otro lado

116

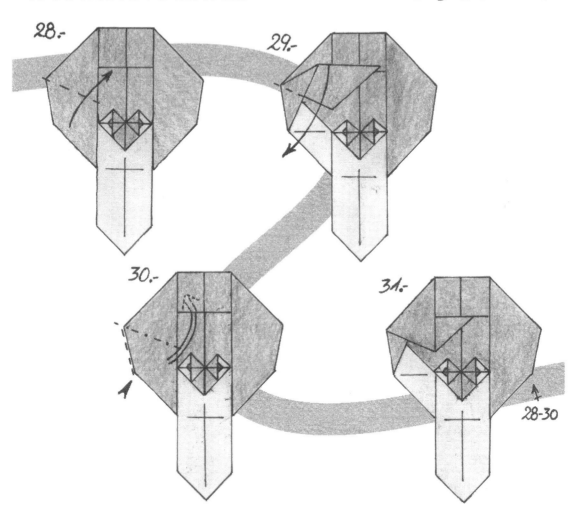

"RANA-MONDADIENTES"

Sergio L. Guarachi V.

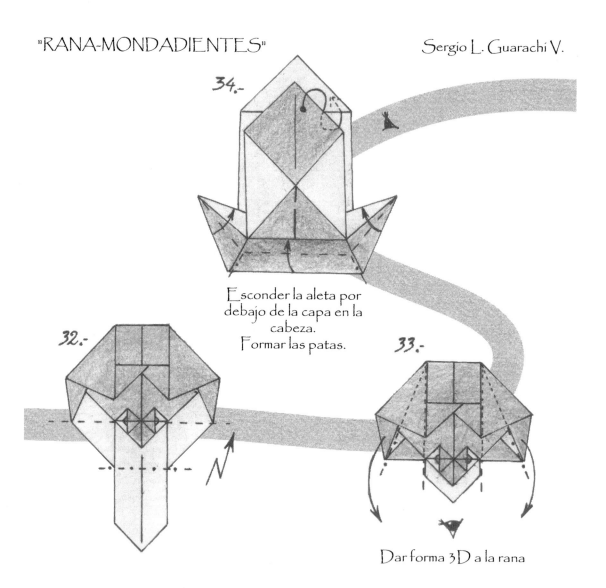

34.-

Esconder la aleta por debajo de la capa en la cabeza.
Formar las patas.

32.-

33.-

Dar forma 3D a la rana

35.-

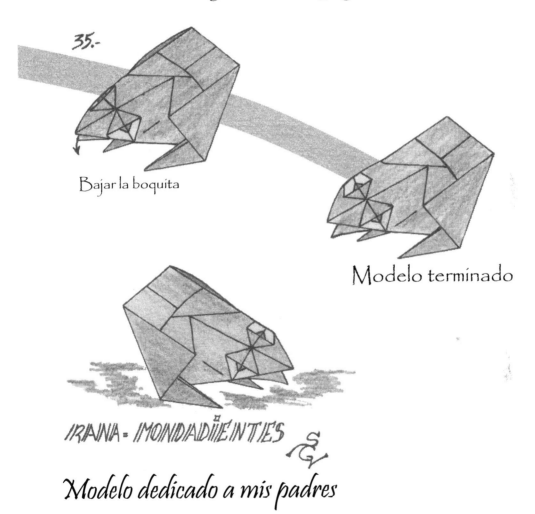

Bajar la boquita

Modelo terminado

RANA - MONDADIENTES

Modelo dedicado a mis padres

Step 8:

For other reasons

Pointed Square

Model: Vincent Achard
Diagrams: Juan Campos & Jens Kober

From a 15x15cm sheet you fold a
5.4x5.4cm square with a 6.2cm tall tip.

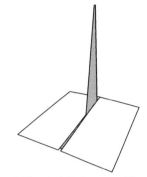

"What is it for" you ask?...
Why don't you take a look
at the last page of the diagrams?

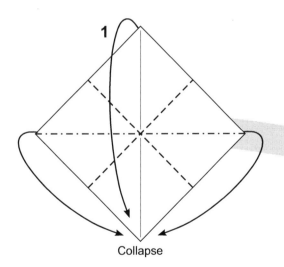

1

Collapse

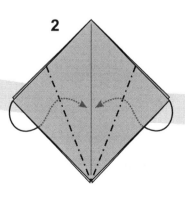

2

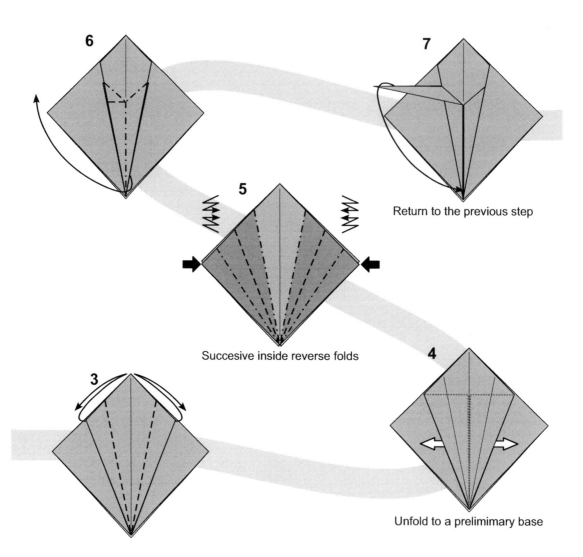

6

7

Return to the previous step

5

Succesive inside reverse folds

3

4

Unfold to a prelimimary base

124

8

Open all the layers

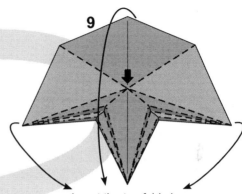

9

Invert the top folds by
pressing a little at the center

10

Close as shown

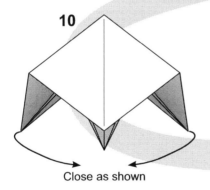

11

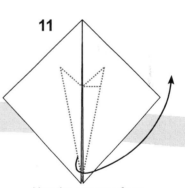

Use the creases from
step 6 to extract the tip

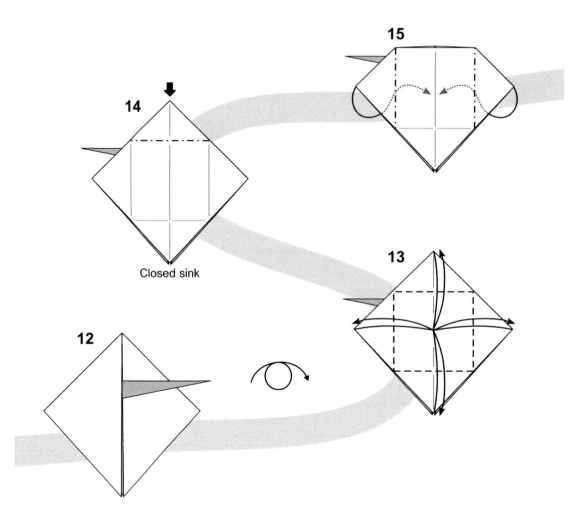

14
Closed sink

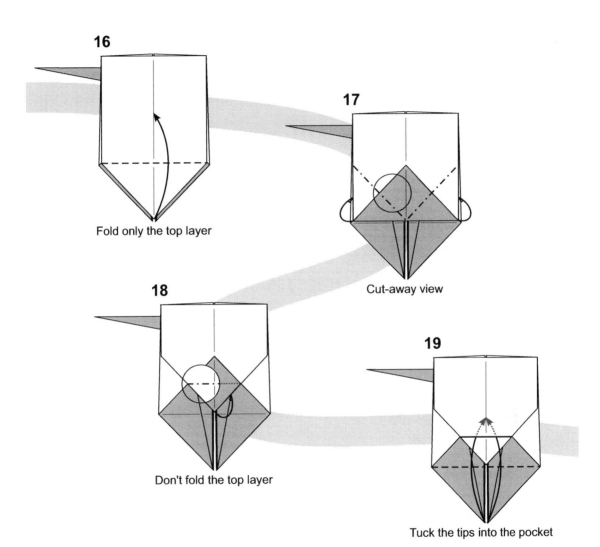

16

Fold only the top layer

17

Cut-away view

18

Don't fold the top layer

19

Tuck the tips into the pocket

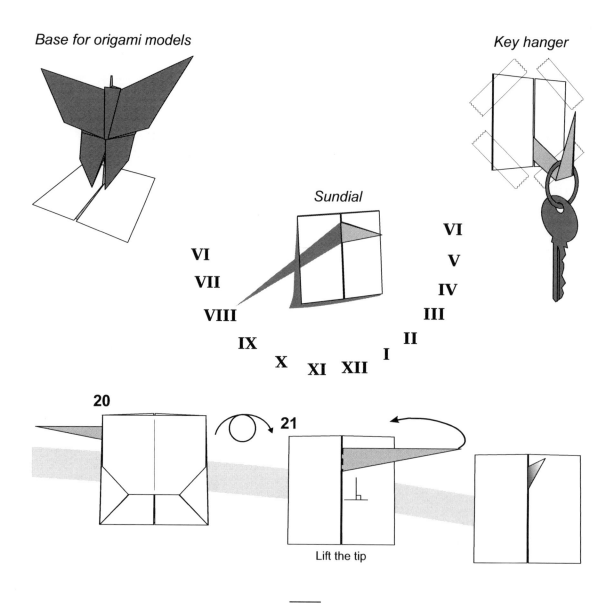

Base for origami models

Key hanger

Sundial

VI
VII
VIII
IX
X   XI   XII

VI
V
IV
III
II
I

20

21

Lift the tip

Voodoo Doll

Design and diagram by Hubert Villeneuve

Recommended starting size :
10cm x 20cm

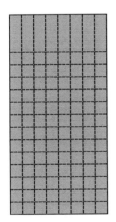

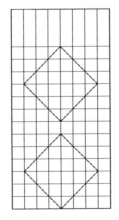

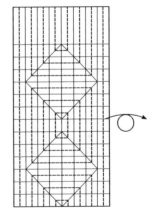

1. Start with a 2:1 rectangle, color face up. Pleat in vertical eighths and horizontal sixteenths, leaving the top untouched.

2. Crease the diagonals.

3. Pleat all current divisions in half as indicated.

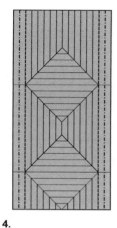

4.

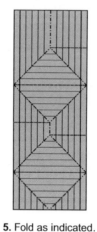

5. Fold as indicated.

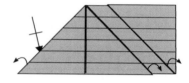

6. Release four trapped corners.

8. Fold one flap to the left while incorporating a reverse fold through all layers.

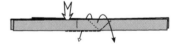

9. Bring the two left flaps down and spread symmetrically.

7. Open sink in and out along the precreases.

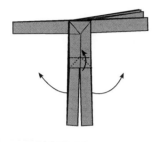

10. Lift the legs up.

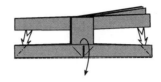

11. Fold the legs down while flattening the ends.

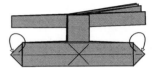

12. Turn one layer of the tip of each leg to the back without flattening them.

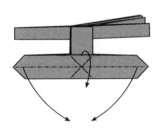

13. Bring the legs down similarly to a preliminary base.

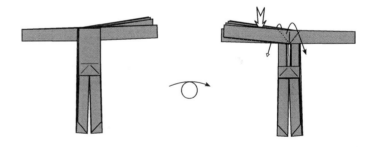

14. Note the tips on each leg.

15. Bring the head flap down and spread symmetrically akin to step 9.

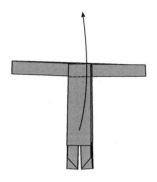

16.

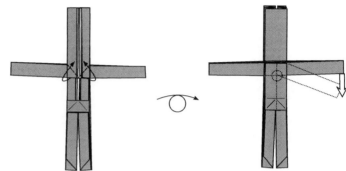

17. Valley fold through all layers. Turn the model over.

18. Pull down the first layer of the arm and flatten it. The base of the neck, the circled part, acts as a pivot.

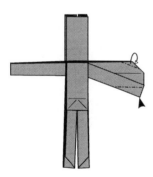

19. Shape the arm.

20. Bring out the longest layer on the leg, the edge of the starting rectangle, and flatten it. This fold should reach the same reference as step 18.

21. Shape the leg.

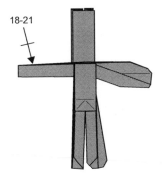

22.

23. Fold and unfold the head in half. This will serve as reference for the next two steps.

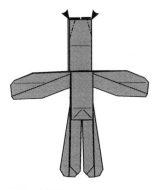

24. Make reverse folds on each layer on the top of the head..

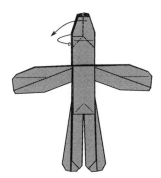

25. Fold the top of the head down to the left, then fold the excess on the left behind. This is similar to a reverse fold.

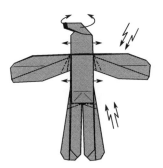

26. Crimp the arms and legs. Spread the layers of the top of the head around. Puff up the head and body.

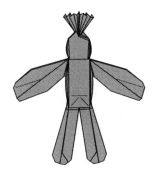

27. Finished model.

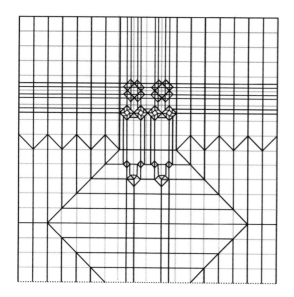

CP CHALLENGE: Face version

The crease pattern on the left is for the face version. You will need a grid of 34x18 instead of 32x16. Fold only along the black lines. The grey lines are only there as reference.

Start with the face by pleating across the initial rectangle. Then, work on the pleat intersections to form the eyes and mouth stitches. Ignore the pleats that reach the edges of the rectangle.

The head pleats will end up slightly longer, so make note of this when following the diagrams.

Good luck!

You can use the voodoo doll as it is intended to. But, would you really *want* to mess this handsome face?

The finished model

Origami is a very diverse practice with a wide variety of themes. One theme that hasn't often been explored is practical origami. Many think of it as exclusively boxes and envelopes. Those are excellent examples but the purpose of the challenge and this book has been to demonstrate that the utility of folded paper can go beyond that in surprising ways.

In my opinion, there are two features that make practical origami different from the more common figurative origami: practical origami is connected with necessities generated from our ordinary lives, so if I need to hang my clothes I could use an origami coat hanger. Besides that, practical origami doesn't depend on the level of similarity between the model and the object it represents. An origami coat hanger doesn't have to resemble the traditional one made of wire; if it allows you to hang your clothes inside the closet in an organized way then it's also a coat hanger.

Having this in mind, when you want to create a new practical model you have two choices, you can try to recreate an existing artifact through origami or you can try to personally figure out how to satisfy an specific need also through origami. Both possibilities can be very challenging; you might come to the conclusion that paper alone isn't enough for the model to work, like in the case of my *Grabber*. When it comes to that many origamists prefer to just discard the project. That's a choice each origami creator must make by him or herself. In your case, what would you do?

Printed in Great Britain
by Amazon